This book is dedicated to
my husband Ted for believing in me,
my daughter Harper Lane for inspiring me, and
my son Theo Michael for encouraging me. – A.M.

I hope this book inspires you to turn any bad situation into an
opportunity to spread kindness. – A.T.

Copyright @2020 by Ashley H. Molnar

Publishing: EmpaThee Lane LLC

Library of Congress Cataloging in Publication Data

EmpaThee Lane LLC books may be purchased for educational, business, or sales
promotional use. For more information, please visit https://www.empatheelane.com/.

ISBN: 978-1-7352842-0-0

what happened to me?

written by
ashley molnar

illustrated by
austen tarabay

Laney headed off to school
her favorite place to be,
where she plays with all her toys
acting silly, fun, and free.

After she finished her morning snack,
she grabbed a toy truck to play.
She loves to push it down the track
and watch it drive away.

Just as she went to send it on back
down through the winding track,
Her classmate Ollie came over and yanked
the truck right behind his back.

They could have played together
and had the very best day.
Instead, Laney walked away so upset,
leaving Ollie alone to play.

The rest of the day, she thought about Ollie
and how he could have been kind.
Instead of grabbing the truck from her hands,
he could have asked...

The next day at school, Laney went to play
and her favorite truck was still there.
She got so excited to drive it again.
To give it up, she didn't dare!

Then Ollie walked over, his eye on the truck,
and Laney was ready this time.
But instead of hiding her truck from him,
she invited him to her playtime.

She remembered the way Ollie made her feel
when he snatched her truck from behind.
She didn't want Ollie to feel how she felt,
and instead, she chose to be kind.

ALWAYS BE KIND

No act of kindness, no matter how small
is ever a waste of your time.
One kind act can change someone's day,
so be kind…

EVERY TIME!

Questions to Ask Your Child

Help your child develop empathy by teaching them how to identify their feelings and the feelings of others.

Start today by asking your child these questions:

1. Laney likes to play with her toys at school. What is your favorite part about school?
2. How do you think Ollie felt when he first saw the truck?
3. How do you think Laney felt when Ollie took the truck from her?
4. Instead of grabbing the truck from Laney, what could Ollie have done?
5. How did it make you feel when you saw Laney was upset? Does it feel good to see others upset? Does it feel good to see others happy?
6. Talk about a time when you have shared with a friend.
7. How did Ollie feel once Laney asked him to play with her?
8. How did Laney feel once she asked Ollie to play with her?
9. Do you think that sharing with others helps you to make friends?
10. What is something kind that you can do for someone today?

About EmpaThee Lane

Ashley Molnar created EmpaThee Lane to publish children's books that teach our youth empathy, how to understand their feelings and the feelings of others, and how to be kind through storytelling.

If we can help our children learn empathy and embed those behaviors at young ages, we have a real shot at changing the world and how we treat each other. Can you think of a better mission than that?

Learn more here: https://www.empatheelane.com/